JOURNEY TOWARD A JOB

Chapter One

Words We Don't Want to Hear

"What do you mean I'm laid off?"

Lisa couldn't believe the words. Laid off, restructured, unemployed – jobless. Well the whole idea of being without a job was okay, but when she thought of not having her job, there was usually a coconut drink and a palm tree in her dream. Not to mention a very fit cabana boy. Shaking her head she realized that this wasn't a dream, it was day time alright, but it was more of a nightmare.

She was five years out of college and within the past year she bought her first home. Okay, it wasn't a stately mansion, but it was a nice two bedroom condo in a nice neighborhood. She decorated it with some stylish furniture from IKEA and some hand me downs provided by her mom and dad. A few candles here, a couple of vases there and it looked like a place she could call home. Whatever you wanted to call it, it was hers. Along with the $1800 a month payment and the empty bank account she now had due to the large down payment. Yep, all hers.

Lisa went home, prepared herself one of those fruity drinks with a little rum in it and sat on her back deck listening to Norah Jones. Good subdued music for a subdued kind of day. It was a gorgeous 78 degree June day in the Mid-West and it felt good to enjoy the blue sky and warm breeze instead of the glare of fluorescent lights and the weekend tales of her cube mate Michael. It may even be warm enough to get her tan started. She wasn't known as a bronze goddess, but a little color certainly wouldn't hurt.

June turned in to July, which turned in to August and then September. The tan was improving each week, but Norah Jones got depressing. She decided that a range of music from Kid Rock to Three Days Grace (ironic group to be listening to with her mortgage and credit cards overdue) would be better to listen to each day on her IPod.

With no job in sight, Lisa decided that she needed to take a more proactive approach if she was going to find a job. She would have to swallow her pride and ask others for help. Depending on help from others was never her strong suit. She enjoyed being self sufficient and this wasn't easy for her, but being self sufficient wasn't going to be possible much longer without an income coming in.

Chapter Two

Dad to the Rescue?

As much as she hated to do so, Lisa went to her dad for advice. He on the other hand was always glad to help; pops did what he could for his little girl. Of course, it's that "little girl" thing that still sat wrong with Lisa in the first place.

The problem that she soon found out is that he hadn't looked for a job himself for over 25 years. Even so, he was willing to give it a try.

"Are you getting enough to eat? You're looking a little thin," her dad asked her.

"Yeah dad, no dad … I mean, I'm eating the same as I always have and haven't lost any weight."

This is how the conversation always seemed to start between the two of them. Or it centered on her love life (or lack there of), or if her car was running fine. I guess it could be worse than having a dad that cares for you, she thought to herself.

The small talk ended and her dad was ready to give some advice to his little *lady bug*. That was his nickname for his only daughter. The advice included; keeping her resume to one page and using heavy cotton paper with a matching envelope when she mails it.

She finished off her Mountain Dew and thanked her dad for the advice. "No problem *lady bug*, good luck out there and keep your spirits up."

Keeping her spirits up was probably the best guidance he provided, she thought to herself, as she walked out the door.

Walking out of her parent's house Lisa thought to herself; well, I already know that a resume can be one or two pages, based on the amount of content and years of experience in a person's career. She already made a resume she was happy with and kept it to just under two pages.

She also knew that mailing resumes went out the way of the last millennium, so that wasn't a concern. She was just glad that pops didn't suggest that she include a picture, health and marriage status as was common when he got his first job. Boy how things have changed.

<u>Chapter Three</u>

Rock the Laptop

After speaking with her dad, Lisa felt like she went through a time warp, so she decided to call her old cube mate Michael. As pathetic as some of his weekend exploits were, he was more in tune with what was currently going on in the world.

Michael also lost his job and he was more than happy to help. He told her stories of the great parties that he went to and said how Twitter, MySpace and Facebook are where it's at. He filled her in on how he combs through job info from his cell or laptop. The added benefit is that he knows where the best local bands are playing too.

This got Lisa excited. It sounded like her way to shop for a job.

Of course, there was one minor problem. Lisa soon found out that Michael has only gone on one interview during the past few months and spent more time connecting with his friends about the local band scene or the latest app for his phone. The job search didn't really seem front and center in his efforts. A new job didn't seem to be his target as it seemed more of an afterthought.

Now she was more disappointed than before, so she decided to grab her laptop and go down to the local coffee shop to be around people. She needed the vibrancy of being around other people, energy to feed off of. She knew that it was good to get out and mingle amongst others instead of staying holed up by herself for too long.

On her way out, she ran in to Eric, her neighbor from the condo complex. Well she didn't really *run* in to Eric. Eric tripped and fell in to Lisa. Embarrassing for Eric, and with how he landed in to her, a little uncomfortable as well.

Eric felt horrible and asked if he could do anything for her. He was a nice guy, but she just wanted to go get an overpriced coffee and chill, so she said so.

"Really, a coffee at 6pm – sounds great to me. My treat" Eric said. Knowing that her purse was near empty and her love for a Venti Vanilla Latte needed to be satisfied, Lisa took Eric up on his offer.

Chapter Four

An Extra Large Java and a Job to Go Please

It was good to laugh again. This is the first time Lisa had spent any significant time with Eric and she found out that he had a nice personality.

She learned that his job was that of a Recruiter. He had a job, but it must be tough during these difficult economic times, with so few companies hiring. Even though these weren't the best of times for him either, he laughed easily and often during their conversation.

"I've seen you around home more often lately" Eric said.

"Yeah, I got laid off a few months back and I haven't been able to find a job yet. Heck, I haven't even had an interview and the weather will be getting colder soon – so improving on my tan will be out of the question."

Upon hearing of Lisa's situation, Eric offered advice and Lisa was a willing ear.

"My biggest problem right now is getting an interview. I think I'd do well if I can get in front of an employer, but I don't know where to start."

With that, Eric apologized since his firm's area of recruiting wasn't a fit for her career, but he had ideas that could help her get an interview.

Eric started off by saying that networking is one of the best ways to find a job. Especially during tough times when the only difference you may offer the potential employer is a common friend or relative.

"Heck, I recommend that you volunteer your time to a local charity or community group while you're out of work. That way you'll keep busy and feel good about yourself, all the while you'll help your community and you may even meet someone that connects you to your next job. It's a win-win situation."

"It's not always easy announcing to the world that you're out of work and need help finding a job"; Eric said "but it is a great way to get back in to the game."

In fact, now they have a site called LinkedIn.com that allows you to set up your background (much like a resume) and *link* or connect with friends, former classmates, former co-workers and relatives. It's like Facebook.com or MySpace.com, but more orientated to the working world. You can announce that you're looking for job opportunities as well.

"Heck, I know many recruiters, both corporate internal recruiters and third party head hunters that use LinkedIn.com as a personal database."

"Just remember" Eric added, "You should still pick up the phone or tell people personally in addition to using LinkedIn.com."

"Wow, it's that easy?" Lisa expressed.

"No, but networking is a start" replied Eric. He went on further to explain that finding a job can be tough and time consuming, but if done right, it can be successful and not take so long.

He went on to discuss job sites like Monster.com, CareerBuilder.com, YahooJobs.com and the many niche sites built around a specific career or industry. One of the best ways to find niche sites is by using Google and exploring the various options. Eric explained that the job board sites have basically taken the place of the local paper.

With that said, depending on your profession, checking out the local paper can still be beneficial. For example, many administrative or manufacturing related jobs still tend to use newspapers – especially smaller, older companies.

Lisa was brimming with ideas at this point. She asked about Job Fairs.

"True, job fairs are built for the purpose of finding candidates, but I'm not a big fan of them." Eric went on to explain about the cattle herd mentality, especially during tough times. Actually, you often don't meet with anyone of relevance when you go to them. On the other hand, if you have the time and energy, it doesn't hurt. "Think of Job Fairs as an option, but not one of your primary strategies."

Another option is a recruiter. "Now…they're not all as good looking and nice as me…"

Eric knew he crossed the line and made it obvious that he was flirting. Of course, that didn't really matter to him, and judging by her reaction, it didn't seem to bother Lisa any either. Many professions use recruiters instead of advertising or in addition to advertising, so finding one is a way to assist in your search.

You don't pay the recruiter. The company works with the recruiter to identify good candidates, help them through the process and it's the company that pays the fee once they hire someone. For many experienced professionals it's an excellent way to get your name out there, get career advice and hopefully get a job.

Eric explained that it's advisable to use two recruiters. You don't want to leave your important job search to one person and their network, but more than two tends to be a waste of everyone's time and efforts start to overlap too much. In the end, you may get less attention by using more than two recruiters. Also, an important element to remember when working with a recruiter is that you should always be asked if your resume can be sent to a company. If the recruiter doesn't follow that process, their integrity should be questioned and I'd advise you to find a different one. Ask friends and co-workers if they know of a good recruiter in your profession.

For some professions, temporary service companies (also known as consulting companies and contract houses depending on the profession) can be useful.

They work differently than a direct hire recruiter in that they would have interim positions available that will have you working through them, not with the end client. These jobs may be weeks, months or years in length. In fact, many of these firms now offer benefits, especially for higher paying long term jobs. Many people have found jobs and advanced their careers starting off in a position as a temporary employee. Going this route also allows you to keep your skills fresh, meet additional people to network with and bring some money in. It's usually a win-win for everyone if you're unemployed.

I'll look in to that so that I can pay the mortgage if I don't find a job soon. Lisa thought to herself.

"Darn, it looks like our coffee is done" Lisa sighed. "Sounds like it's time to eat then. I know of a little café down the road that has a great panini." Eric led the way, both of them forgetting that they just met for the first time this afternoon.

<u>Chapter Five</u>

Can't Start Until You Take Step One

"I can't let you loose on the world with the limited information I provided," Eric explained.

"Limited? My head is swimming already" she replied.

"That's just it. We need to put a focused plan in place."

"Whoa, wait a minute. I'm not a real structured person and I'm uncomfortable trying to be someone whom I'm not."

With a nice soft laugh, Eric assured Lisa that he wouldn't turn her into a robot. He went on to use the analogy that it's much easier to hit a target when you're aiming at it, instead of spraying bullets in a random direction.

With a little reluctance, Lisa agreed to continue, knowing that Eric had her success in mind with his process.

He asked Lisa a few questions about her background making mental notes along the way. He then inquired about what she wanted to do going forward in her career and what was most important to her from a career perspective.

For instance, was it money, was it the location of the job, or was it the opportunity to climb the corporate ladder? Perhaps it had to do with the culture of the company, the ability to learn or the work / life balance provided?

Everyone has a list of what's important to them and she had to determine that for herself. He explained that this is perhaps the most important step. Step One…self evaluation.

Knowing what you're capable of and what you desire to do on a job. Then compare those items to a realistic set of jobs that exist.

Do you need additional credentials or education? Will your past experience support the direction you want to head? If not, then there may be intermediate career positions or educational steps you must take before being able to obtain your final career goal.

"The honey ham and capicola panini is outstanding" Eric offered, but Lisa still stuck with something that had bean sprouts in it.

Yes, there is a difference between men and women Eric thought.

By this point in the conversation Eric was able to guide Lisa through where she should start looking for jobs and which types of jobs she should target.

One mistake many people make is when they shotgun their resume to any posting or company. The theory they stand by is that some angel at the firm is going to see the resume and even though it has nothing to do with their area, the *angel* will search out a job for them.

She could see that this was an irritant to him, so she let him continue.

"This is a waste of time and energy on everyone's part." Eric huffed. It's very rude to waste other's time and it is a very unsuccessful approach.

Lisa understood the point and honed in on the career path she was looking for and the types of jobs to get right now to obtain her goals. One of the additional benefits of this approach is that Lisa was able to use specific niche job boards.

Eric also explained that she may want to target specific companies in her geographic and career area and check their web sites each week. Most mid-sized and large companies now post their jobs on their own web site. Often before sending them out to the job boards, meaning your resume is seen before the masses get involved. In fact, if they get a good enough response, they may not advertise to the general population at all.

Companies also like candidates whom target their company to work for, versus the candidate that will take whichever job is presented first. They are looking for a long term employee and want to invest in one who wants to invest in their career.

This brought to mind a client of Eric's who always asks her candidates; "You explained to me why you are looking for another position, but why specifically do you want to work HERE?" Over the years Eric saw many a good candidate get stuck on that one and not proceed any further.

"The sandwich was great and the help you've provided me was awesome!" Lisa extolled. Eric didn't mind, he was starting to like Lisa and he would help in any way possible.

Chapter Six

Testing the Waters

Lisa followed Eric's advice or most of it since she got lost in the thought of his eyes every time she went back to their conversation. The thought of his deep brown eyes did tend to get in the way of a few details.

After a few weeks Lisa lined up two interviews for jobs she was interested in and with companies that were of interest to her.

One interview was Friday and the other one will be on Tuesday of next week. She felt like things were turning out for the better already.

She saw Eric every so often around the condo and they would have the occasional coffee together. The relationship didn't seem to progress, but at least she found a new friend. Besides, she had the challenge of finding a job in a tough economy. Perhaps it wasn't time to start a serious relationship.

The interview on Friday morning was with a Human Resources Representative and it lasted about 30 minutes.

She left feeling that she wasn't able to make a connection with the Rep and never got in to a flow to explain why she would be good for the job. To be honest, Lisa didn't feel real confident going in to the interview and based on a self evaluation, she didn't feel real confident now that she was leaving the interview.

As she got in her car and cranked up the music in her Aveo she wondered what she should do next.

One answer came to her immediately. Perhaps it was time to move a little more aggressively with Eric. At that moment she decided that she'd call to see if he was available for dinner.

"Oh, hi Lisa" he answered on his cell. "Sorry, but I can't do dinner tonight."

Before she could do the back stroke, disconnect and save face somehow, Eric continued; "but I'd love to meet for dinner Saturday night."

Hmm…maybe this part of her life was turning around as well she thought to herself. A smile formed on her face and her mind was suddenly clearer than it had been all morning.

Chapter Seven

Thai for Two

"Pad Thai – *hot* with pork" was ordered by Eric in a confident and assured tone.

It wasn't as easy for Lisa since the whole Thai food experience was new to her, she just ordered something called *K4* adding that she wanted chicken and asked if it could be made *mild.*

As with other aspects of her life, she was tentative when it came to things she didn't know. Heck, she was often tentative even after learning and appreciating those things. Anyway, she was a little afraid of the spices that she'd heard about in Thai food. Eric reassured her that ordering Thai food *mild* wasn't all that different than ordering Chinese. She was comfortable with that explanation and told him that she was willing to try a bite of his meal, if it was alright with him.

After a few jokes about the appetizer chips resembling Styrofoam, Lisa preceded to tell Eric about her interview Friday morning.

He listened attentively staring into those beautiful blue grey eyes of hers.

She finally admitted that she needed more assistance and since the last talk with him was so helpful, she was wondering if he could work his magic again.

Upon hearing those words his chest puffed out and he jokingly replied; "So, you're just using me for my brain?"

He had a slightly mischievous look on his face and let her know that; "this is going to cost you. I'm cheap, but I'm not free."

Lisa started to blush, but Eric immediately put her at ease and started talking her through the process.

"Well, the first thing you should do is prepare yourself for the interview. Heck a professional football player practices all week to play several hours on Sunday."

I did, she replied, stating how she looked the company up on-line and found out about their products and services.

"That's good, did you do anything else?"

Based on her blank stare, he assumed not and continued.

Looking at the company's web site is a good start. Also, use Google to look up information about the company and for the latest in news about them.

You'd hate to enter a situation where the company just went through a traumatic event and you weren't aware of it.

Likewise, there could be a new product or community event that they're proud of and if you miss out on the opportunity to discuss it, brownie points may be lost. Review their products or services; know their revenue and where locations are as well. Not that you have to memorize the information or repeat it in the interview like a robot, but a general background knowledge may be useful as they're talking about their company.

Another way to use the information is by dropping in a few comments throughout the conversation which will show that you know about their Swedish subsidiary or the education program that they are sponsoring. These comments will usually earn bonus points for effort if nothing else.

Beyond researching via Google and the company web site, it's also important to think about questions you'll ask them as well as how to respond to questions that they may ask you.

For instance, most people are comfortable when asked to name a strength of theirs. On the other hand, how comfortable are you if the human resources representative asks you to name a weakness, or an area to improve?

That line of questions can be difficult for most people. Answer the wrong way, such as mentioning your lack of attention to detail for a job that needs it and you'll be done in her eyes before you really get going. Likewise, not answering at all or having that *deer in the headlights* look can be just as negative.

"Well, what do you recommend then Eric?" At least he knew by her question that she was awake and paying attention. Sometimes he felt like he was rambling. Eric continued.

The best way to answer that question is to bring up a weakness of your past, but one that doesn't relate to the job you're interviewing for.

Another approach is to answer it with a solution in place. Something like; I've always been very hard on myself to accomplish the various goals and deadlines I've set. During my last job at XYZ Company I found the solution for that issue. It was a high pressure position and I got very use to the chaotic work flow. In fact, even though I'm still working on that part of my personality, I tend to enjoy that atmosphere now. Eric reminded Lisa that you never want to lie…but that doesn't mean you can't turn your response of a tough question in to a positive.

This is where practice comes in to play. Take time with a friend to respond to potential interview questions. You can get lists of questions from various internet sites. Provide the list for your friend and go through responses. It's even better if you have a tape recorder available so that you can play back the answers in private.

Eric started writing and listed out some common questions and responses so that Lisa could be prepared:

- Why do you think you're the best person for this job? *(Hit on your experience and personality traits that match up with someone who would be successful in the job)*

- The job requires a background in X, and I don't see that on your resume – why do you think you're qualified? *(hint – you got this far, there must be a reason)*

- You have a period of six months on your resume without a job, what happened during that time? *(Just tell the truth...)*

- This position requires the ability to negotiate. Can you tell me of a time that you lead a negotiation process, whether it was in a work or a personal situation? *(This is called a behavioral question and requires a real-life scenario to speak about)*

- What is the biggest accomplishment from your past job *(This is an excellent question, because it opens the door to brag about yourself – so be ready to light the world on fire!)*

Eric continued to write down more questions. "Okay, okay, I think I have enough." Lisa appreciated the help but she probably had enough ammunition for this portion of the interview.

"You also said that I should have questions prepared to ask in the interview?"

"Yes!" Eric jumped in. This not only shows interest on your part, but it is a great way to find out more about the company and the job so that you can evaluate whether or not it's where you want to spend 40 plus hours each week.

"For instance, ask how long the person interviewing you has been with the company. If it's only been a short while, ask what brought them to XYZ. If they've been there awhile, ask what they like best about working at XYZ."

Eric went on to explain that this has been one of his favorite questions because it personalizes the conversation. You allow them to brag about the place where they work allowing the interview to become more of a conversation. Remember, most people want to let others know that they made a good decision themselves.

"In fact, I just read some survey results today from the Society of Human Resource Management. In that survey 54% of Human Resource professionals said that they made the final decision to hire based on chemistry." Eric went on to say, "I guess it's important to have a give and take conversation instead of just letting them do the talking."

"Heck, if they can't come up with something good to say – that's a sign that perhaps this isn't the right company for you. Run, and run fast from that company. Otherwise you may get stuck in a company like the one in that old Tom Hanks movie, *Joe Versus the Volcano*. I still have nightmares about the flickering fluorescent lights and the abusive boss."

Lisa had to giggle a little over that obscure reference.

Eric continued, "Another thing to remember is that interviews often consist of meeting multiple people in individual settings. A key to remember is to ask each and every one of the people several questions. There are multiple reasons for doing so."

"First, you don't want the later participants to walk away thinking that you don't care just because your questions were answered by the first or second person in the interview process."

"Likewise, if you ask the same question of multiple people it's a great way to paint a picture from different perspectives. The same question will probably garner different responses from the immediate supervisor versus the executive or co-worker or the human resources representative. As the saying goes, information is king. This is a great time to gather information about your potential future employer."

Again, Eric wrote down some other common questions to ask;

- What is the training like? *(Just make sure you don't focus too much on what you don't know)*

- Assuming I do well, what kind of career path can I expect? *(Don't focus too much on a future job while demonstrating that you don't want the role you're interviewing for).*

- I see you have a new product out, how do you think that will affect this group?

- What are your expectations for the person that gets this job?

- What is the most important trait in the person you want to hire?

At this stage, Eric brought up common interview guidance so that he didn't overlook anything.

"When asking questions, the ones you want to stay away from, until they bring them up have to do with compensation, benefits and time off." You may be curious about those types of questions but asking them too early in the process will send a signal that you're more concerned about what the company can do for you instead of how your employment will not only make you successful or happy, but also be beneficial for the company.

In most jobs, companies would prefer that you focus on the bigger picture instead of details. Taking the other approach can make you look like a mercenary. If you come to a job only for the money, it makes sense that you will leave the first chance you have to make more money elsewhere. There is a difference between being paid fair and someone who continuously bids themselves out to the highest bidder.

"Wow, you've given me so much to think about" Lisa sighed.

"Wait, I'm not done" Eric replied. Remember, always show up early in case of traffic problems, but don't announce yourself until about 5 minutes prior. To come earlier can be viewed as rude by some people. Dress the part, conservative and professional attire is almost always the best way to go. Even many companies that are business casual expect you to show up on the first interview in a business suit. If they ask you back for a second interview, ask your contact person what the proper attire is for the second meeting. Another item to remember is confidence. A confident person will almost always win out over an equally qualified candidate that is nervous or unprepared. Finally, my last piece of advice is to show desire. Not desperation, but a genuine desire for the job. Yes, even hiring managers don't like getting turned down. Once again, if there are two equal candidates, the one that shows honest desire in working for this specific company will win every time.

Lisa interrupted; "Your noodles must be cold by now, I'm so sorry." She had time to finish her rice dish, which was pretty good she thought, but Eric's food seemed to barely have a dent in it because he was talking so much.

"My fault" Eric said. "I want you to do well so much, I forgot my manners and rambled. Do you have any questions about what I spoke about?"

"Nope – I'm going to kick some ass on my next interview!" Lisa showed confidence that seemed to be lacking previously. Eric was sure that she would do well. Heck…*he* was sold.

<u>Chapter Eight</u>

Crying over Spilled Milk

Eric was walking up his condo steps when he almost got tackled by Lisa. She was laughing and in her excitement to hug him, she bumped the groceries he was holding. Eggs broke, a wine bottle smashed against the floor and even the lid on the milk container came off producing a white waterfall stream down the steps.

"I'm sooooo sorry."

He would have believed her, but the smile on her face said otherwise. "I'm glad you're happy, what's up?"

"I got it! I got it!" She was still bouncing around like a teenage girl who had just been asked to the prom by the cutest guy in the school. "The second company I interviewed with called me back today and offered me the job!"

"That's excellent! Really...but can I put my groceries away? Or what's left of them anyway."

They picked up the scattered groceries and headed in to his condo. He grabbed a rag for the milk and wine that had spilled, and a broom and dustpan for the broken glass. Together they picked up the mess by the stairs.

"I'd love to celebrate with you, but my bottle of Argentine Malbec will be tough to drink since it's all over the steps."

"Absolutely I want to celebrate! You've been so helpful to me I don't know how to repay you."

"Not needed" he replied, though some thoughts were going through his head. He was a guy after all and he liked Lisa from the moment they met.

"If you don't mind a Pinot Noir, I have a bottle in my condo that I can bring right over."

"A Burgundy it is" Eric replied referring to the French region where Pinot Noir grapes are made into the traditional light red wine. He left the door open so that she could return with the bottle. In the mean time, he got a couple of crystal wine glasses out. No mason jars tonight!

Chapter Nine

The Tough Part...

Eric turned on the stereo with an Otis Redding CD quietly playing in the background. Something about (*Sittin' On) the Dock of the Bay* always mellowed him out, in a good way.

Lisa spoke of how the company wanted three business references, not professors or family. She already got permission from four previous supervisors and co-workers so that wasn't an issue. She told Eric how they did a drug test and since doing drugs wasn't her style, she had no concerns with that part of the process either. The Manager said they even searched for Lisa on the various social networks like many companies are doing now and nothing negative came up. She went back in a second time to speak to her future boss and after about 20 minutes of small talk and discussion about how Lisa would fit in, the lady gave Lisa the offer. It was slightly higher than what she was making previously, and she wouldn't have to travel as much. Not only that, but the long term outlook of the company and her role are both very exciting.

As she continued talking, Lisa found herself curled up on the couch next to Eric with the fire blazing in the background and a glass of wine in her hand. She felt very comfortable in this position.

"I hate to ruin the mood, but you know, now comes the tough part." Eric said.

"Oh my gosh – what could it be? You've been so helpful – what did I miss?" She sounded somewhat exasperated.

"The tough part is - now you have to go to work early each morning and do well – getting the job is only the start!"

A sigh of relief went across Lisa's face and she gave Eric a gentle jab to the arm. "You had me scared there for a moment."

"The job-that's it? – Don't worry, after looking for one, actually doing the job will be the easy part."

About the Author

Jeff Farrington, a 20 year veteran of the staffing industry, earned both a Bachelor's in Business Administration and a Master's of Science in Management degree. Jeff joined the staffing industry after becoming a Manager at a technology company leading a large staff in an accounting and customer service setting. Within the staffing industry his experience has ranged from sales and recruiting in a temporary staffing setting to direct hire recruiting and leadership roles up to and including that of Vice President of an $800 million, national, specialized staffing firm. Five years ago Jeff created a new staffing company based in Michigan. This firm has grown to provide many Fortune 1000 firms with direct hire recruiting and staffing services. The firm, Dynamic Recruiters, Inc. has operations in several states and works with professionals in the areas of Accounting, Finance, Information Technology, Engineering and Supply Chain Management. Jeff and his wife of 23 years, Diana, have two fantastic teenage sons; Mitch and Nick.